AF120578

k-pop

A short encyclopedia

from Wikipedia, the Free encyclopedia

Edited by Jee-Eun Park

CONTENTS

CHAPTER 1 : K-POP DEFINITION AND CHARACTERISTICS ... 3

CHAPTER 2 : ORIGINS OF K-POP 7

CHAPTER 3 : THE K-POP INDUSTRY 19

CHAPTER 4 : K-POP WORLDWIDE POPULARITY 25

CHAPTER 5 : DID YOU KNOW THAT...?
20 INTERESTING FACTS ABOUT K-POP 37

KOREAN POP STARS 41

K-POP ARTISTS DICTIONARY 47

SOURCES 57

K-Pop

K-Pop. A short encyclopedia.

Content from the K-Pop entry in Wikipedia, the Free Encyclopedia :
Wikipedia contributors. "K-pop." Wikipedia, The Free Encyclopedia., 1 Jan. 2017. Web. 11 Jan. 2017.< https://en.wikipedia.org/wiki/K-pop >

Book and Cover design by William Labelle
ISBN: 9782322132904
First Edition: January 2017

Chapter One

K-pop definition and characteristics

"K-pop is a fusion of synthesized music, sharp dance routines and fashionable and colorful outfits…" — *INA Global*

K-pop (an abbreviation of Korean pop; Hangul: 케이팝) is a musical genre originating in South Korea that is characterized by a wide variety of audiovisual elements. Although it comprises all genres of "popular music" within South Korea, the term is more often used in a narrower sense to describe a modern form

K-Pop

of South Korean pop music covering a range of styles including dance-pop, pop ballad, electropop, R&B and hip-hop music. The genre emerged with one of the earliest K-pop groups, Seo Taiji and Boys, forming in 1992. Their experimentation with different styles of music "reshaped Korea's music scene". As a result, the integration of foreign musical elements has now become common practice in the K-pop industry. K-pop entered the Japanese market at the turn of the 21st century and rapidly grew into a subculture among teenagers and young adults of East and Southeast Asia. With the advent of online social networking services, the current global spread of K-pop and Korean entertainment known as the Korean Wave is seen in Latin America, India, North Africa, the Middle East, and elsewhere in the Western world.

Characteristics

Audiovisual content

Although K-pop generally refers to South Korean popular music, some consider it to be an all-encompassing genre ex- hibiting a vast spectrum of musical and visual elements. The French Institut national de l'audiovisuel defines K-pop as a 'fusion of synthesized music, sharp dance routines and fashionable, colorful outfits'. Songs typically consist of one or a mixture of pop, rock, hip hop, R&B and electronic music genres.

Systematic training of artists

Management agencies in South Korea offer binding contracts to potential artists, sometimes at a young age. Trainees live together in a regulated environment and spend many hours a day learning music, dance, foreign languages and other skills in preparation for their debut. This "robotic" system of training is often criticized by Western media outlets. In 2012, The Wall Street Journal reported that the cost of training one "idol" under S.M. Entertainment averaged US$3 million.

Hybrid genre and transnational values

K-pop is a cultural product that features, as JungBong Choi and Maliangkay Roald says "values, identity and meanings that go beyond their strictly commercial value" (*K-pop – The International Rise of the Korean Music Industry.* New York: Routledge, 2015). It is characterized by a mixture of Western sounds with an Asian aspect of performance. It has been remarked that there is a "vision of modernization" inherent in Korean pop culture. For some, the transnational values of K-pop are responsible for its success. A commentator at the University of California has said that "contemporary Korean pop culture is built on [...] transnational flows [...] taking place across, beyond, and outside national and institutional boundaries." Some examples of the transnational values inherent in K-pop that may appeal to those from different ethnic, national, and religious backgrounds include a dedication to high-quality output and presentation of idols, as well as their work ethic and polite social demeanour, made possible by the training period.

* * *

A short encyclopedia

Chapter Two

Origins of K-Pop

"*From this unpromising position South Korea managed to charge past Japan to become Asia's foremost trendsetter ...*" — *The Economist, Aug. 9th 2014*

The history of Korean popular music can be traced bac to 1885 when an American missionary, Henry Appenzeller, began teaching American and British folk songs at a school. These songs were called changga in Korean, and they were typically based on a popular Western melody sung with Korean lyrics. For example, the song "Oh My Darling, Clementine" became known as "Simcheongga". During the Japanese rule (1910–1945) the popularity of changga songs rose as Koreans expressed their feelings against Japanese oppression through music. One of the most popular songs was "Huimangga" (희망가, The Song of Hope). The Japanese confiscated the existing changga collections and published lyrics books of their own. The first known Korean pop album was "Yi Pungjin Sewol" (This Tumultuous Time), by Park Chae-seon and Lee Ryu-saek in 1925, which contained popular songs translated from Japanese. The first pop song written by a Korean composer is thought to be "Nakhwayusu" (낙화유수, Fallen Blossoms on Running Water) sung by Lee Jeong-suk in 1929. In the mid-1920s, Japanese composer Masao Koga mixed traditional Korean music with Gospel music that American Evangelists introduced in the 1870s. This type of music became known as Enka in Japan, and later in Korea as Trot (Korean: "트로트").

A short encyclopedia

1940s-1960s: the rise of the Western culture in Korean popular music

After the Korean Peninsula was partitioned into North and South following its liberation in 1945 from Japanese occupation, Western culture was introduced into South Korea on a small scale, with a few Western-styled bars and clubs playing Western music. After the Korean War (1950–53) U.S. troops remained in South Korea for protection. With the continued presence of the U.S. military during this time, American and world culture spread in South Korea and Western music gradually became more accepted. The United Service Organizations made it possible for several prominent figures of American entertainment, like Marilyn Monroe and Louis Armstrong to visit the soldiers stationed in Korea. These visits prompted attention from the Korean public. In 1957 the American Forces Korea Network radio started its broadcast, spreading the popularity of Western music. American music started influencing Korean music, as pentatony was gradually replaced by heptachords and popular songs started to be modeled after American ones. In the 1960s, the development of LP records and improvements in recording technology led to the pursuit of diverse voice tones. Many singers sang for the

K-Pop

American troops, usually in dedicated clubs, the number of which rose to 264. They performed various genres like country music, blues, jazz and rock & roll. The South Korean economy started blooming and popular music followed the trend, spread by the first commercial radio stations. Korean cinema also began to develop and Korean musicians began performing to wider audiences. When Beatlemania reached the shores of Korea the first local rock bands appeared, the first of which is said to be Add4, a band founded in 1962. The first talent contest for rock bands in Seoul was organized in 1968. Besides rock and pop, trot songs remained popular. Some Korean singers gained international popularity. The Kim Sisters, Yoon Bok-hee and Patti Kim were the first singers to debut in such countries as Vietnam and United States. The Kim Sisters became the first Korean group to release an album in the United States, performing in Las Vegas and appearing several times on Ed Sullivan's TV show. Han Myeong Suk's 1961 song "The Boy in The Yellow Shirt" was covered by French singer Yvette Giraud and was also popular in Japan.

A short encyclopedia

1970s: Hippie and folk influences in Korean popular music

At the end of the 1960s Korean pop music underwent another transformation. More and more musicians were university students and graduates who were heavily influenced by American culture and lifestyle (including the hippie movement) and made lighthearted music unlike their predecessors, who were influenced by war and Japanese oppression. The younger generation opposed the Vietnam War as much as American hippies did, which resulted in the Korean government banning songs with more liberal lyrics. In spite of this, folk-influenced pop remained popular among the youth, and local television channel MBC organised a music contest for university students in 1977. This was the foundation of several modern music festivals. One of the leading figures of the era was Han Dae-soo, who was raised in the United States and influenced by Bob Dylan, Leonard Cohen and John Lennon. Han's song "Mul jom juso" (물 좀 주소, Give Me Water) became iconic among young people in Korea. His daring performances and unique singing style often shocked the public and later he was banned from performing in Korea. Han moved to New

York City and pursued his musical career there, only returning to his home country in the 1990s. Other notable singers of the period include Song Chang-sik, Young Nam-cho and Hee Eun-yang.

1980s: The era of sweet pop

The 1980s saw the rise of ballad singers after Lee Gwang-jo's 1985 album "You're Too Far Away to Get Close to" (가까이 하기엔 너무 먼 당신, Gakkai Hagien Neomu Meon Dangsin) sold more than 300,000 copies. Other popular ballad singers included Lee Moon-se (이문세) and Byun Jin-seob (변진섭), nicknamed the "Prince of Ballads". One of the most sought-after ballad composers of the era was Lee Young-hoon (이영훈), whose songs were compiled into a modern musical in 2011 titled Gwanghwamun Yeonga (광화문 연가, Gwanghwamun's Song). The Asia Music Forum was launched in 1980, with representatives from five different Asian countries competing in the event. Korean singer Cho Yong-pil won first place and went on to have a successful career, performing in Hong Kong and Japan. His first album Chang bakkui yeoja (창 밖의 여자,

Woman outside the window) was a hit and he became the first Korean singer to take to the stage at Carnegie Hall in New York. Cho's musical repertoire included rock, dance, trot and folk pop.

1990s: the rise of modern K-pop

In the 1990s, Korean pop musicians incorporated American popular music styles like rap, rock and techno in their music. In 1992 the emergence of Seo Taiji & Boys marked a revolutionary moment in the history of K-pop. The trio debuted on MBC's talent show with their song "Nan Arayo" (난 알아요, I Know) and got the lowest rating from the jury; however, the song and album of the same name became so successful that it paved the way for other songs of the same format. The song's success was attributed to its new jack swing-inspired beats and memorable chorus, as well as innovative lyrics which dealt with the problems of Korean society. Their footsteps were followed by a wave of successful hip hop and R&B artists like Yoo Seung-jun, Jinusean, Deux, 1TYM and Drunken Tiger. In 1995, South Korean record producer Lee Soo-man founded the entertainment company, S.M. Entertainment. Former Seo Taiji & Boys Yang Hyun-suk's member formed YG entertainment in 1996, as did South Korean K-pop singer Park Jin-young established JYP Entertainment in 1997. Idol bands (young boybands or girlbands) formed, inspired by Seo Taiji & Boys, to cater for a growing teenage audience. H.O.T. was one of the first idol boybands, debuting in 1996. Their success was followed by that of bands like Sechs Kies, S.E.S., Fin.K.L, NRG, Baby V.O.X., Diva, Shinhwa and g.o.d. The 1990s were also a successful period for underground music clubs and punk rock bands such as Crying Nut. The 1997 Asian financial crisis prompted South Korean entertainers to look for new markets: H.O.T. released a Mandarin-language album and Diva released an English-language album in Taiwan.

21st century: The Korea Wave (or 'Hallyu') area

K-pop's increasing popularity forms part of Hallyu, or the Korean Wave, which refers to the popularity of South Korean culture in other countries. K-pop is increasingly making appearances on Western charts such as Billboard. The development of online social media has been a vital tool for the Korean music industry in reaching a wider audience. By the beginning of the 21st century, the K-pop idol groups that had seen success in the 90's were on the decline. H.O.T. disbanded in 2001, while other groups like Sechs Kies, S.E.S., Fin.K.L, Shinhwa, and g.o.d became inactive by 2005. Solo singers like BoA and Rain grew in success. However, the successes of TVXQ and SS501 after their debuts in 2003 and 2005, respectively, marked the resurgence of idol groups to Korean entertainment and the growth of K-pop as part of "Hallyu." The birth of second-generation K-pop was followed with the successful debuts of Super Junior (2005), Big Bang (2006), Wonder Girls (2007), Girls' Generation (2007), and Kara (2007). During the beginning of the 21st century, K-pop idols began receiving success elsewhere in Asia: in 2002, Baby V.O.X.'s single "Coincidence" became popular in many Asian countries after it was released and promoted during the World Cup in South Korea. BoA became the first K-pop singer to reach No. 1 on the Japanese Oricon music chart and shortly afterwards, Rain had a sold-out concert to an audience of 40,000 fans in Beijing. In 2003, Baby V.O.X. topped the Chinese music charts with their Chinese single "I'm Still Loving You" from their third album Devotion, the first idol group to do so, creating a huge fanbase in China. They also charted in various music charts in Thailand. TVXQ marked the rise of K-pop boy bands in Japan. In 2008, their single "Purple Line" made TVXQ the first foreign boy band and second Korean artist after BoA to top the Oricon music chart. Since the mid-2000s, a huge portion of the East Asian music market has been dominated by K-pop. In 2008, South Korea's cultural exports (including television dramas and computer games) rose to US$2 billion, maintaining an annual growth rate of over 10%. That year, Japan accounted for almost 68% of all K-pop export revenues, ahead of China (11.2%) and the United States (2.1%). The sale of concert tickets proved to be a lucrative business; TVXQ's Tohoshinki Live Tour in Japan sold over 850,000 tickets at an average cost of US$109 each, generating a total of US$92.6 million in revenues. Elsewhere in the world, the genre has rapidly grown in success, especially after Psy's "Gangnam Style" music video was the first YouTube video to reach one billion views, achieving widespread coverage in mainstream media. As of November 2016, the video has 2.7 billion views. Although several attempts have been made by entertainment companies (with idols such as BoA, Wonder Girls, and CL releasing English-language singles) at breaking into the English-language market, these have not faced overall success. As part of the Korean Wave K-pop has been embraced by the South Korean government as a tool for soft power abroad, particularly towards overseas youth. In 2014 The Economist dubbed Korean pop culture "Asia's foremost trendsetter".

***

K-Pop

NOTES
....
....
....
....
....
....
....
....

A short encyclopedia

Chapter Three

The K-pop industry

"No pain, no gain, I'm fuelled with caffeine called pain" — B.A.P, Young, Wild & Free

K-pop has spawned an entire industry encompassing music production houses, event management companies, music distributors, and other merchandise and service providers. The three biggest companies in terms of sales and revenue are S.M. Entertainment, YG Entertainment and JYP Entertainment, often referred to as the 'Big Three'. These record labels also function as representative agencies for their artists. They are responsible for recruiting, financing, training, and marketing new artists as well as managing their musical activities and public relations. Currently, the agency with the greatest market share is S.M. Entertainment. In 2011, together with Star J Entertainment, AM Entertainment, and Key East, the Big Three companies founded the joint management company United Asia Management.

Sales and market value

In 2009, DFSB Kollective became the first distributor of K-pop on iTunes. In 2011, 1,100 albums were released in South Korea. The hip-hop genre had the most representation, at two-thirds of the total albums. One-third of the albums were from a variety of other genres, including rock, modern folk, and crossover. In 2012, the average cost of obtaining a K-pop song in South Korea amounted to US$0.10 for a single download, or $0.002

when streamed online. In the first half of 2012, according to Billboard, the Korean music industry grossed nearly US$3.4 billion- a 27.8% increase on the previous year- and was recognized by Time magazine as "South Korea's Greatest Export".

Record charts

Korean record charts include the Korea K-Pop Hot 100 and the Gaon Singles Chart. Recently, some K-pop records have appeared on the Oricon Albums Chart of Japan and the Billboard Hot 100 of the United States. In May 2014, EXO became the third K-pop act to enter the Billboard 200 that year after 2NE1, Girls' Generation and Wonder Girls were the first K-Pop act to chart on Billboard 100.

Television

The Korean music industry has spawned numerous related reality TV shows, including talent shows such as Superstar K and K-pop Star, specialist rap competition Show Me The Money and its female counterpart Unpretty Rapstar, and many 'survival' shows, which commonly pit trainees against each other in order to form a new idol group. Examples of survival shows include Jellyfish Entertainment's MyDOL, which formed the boy group VIXX; YG Entertainment's WIN: Who Is Next, which formed the boy group WINNER; MIX&MATCH, which formed iKON; JYP Entertainment's SIXTEEN, which formed girl group Twice; Starship Entertainment's No.Mercy, which formed boy group Monsta X; and most recently Mnet's Produce 101, which formed girl group I.O.I.

Appeal and fan base

Not all K-pop fans are young females, although most are; in 2012 New York magazine interviewed male adult Girls' Generation fans, who admitted to liking the group for its members' looks and personalities, citing the members' humility and friendliness towards the fans. Many fans travel overseas to see their idols on tour, and tourists commonly visit Korea from Japan and China to see K-pop concerts. A K-pop tour group from Japan had more than 7,000 fans fly to Seoul to meet boy band JYJ in 2012, and during JYJ's concert in Barcelona in 2011, fans from many parts of the world camped overnight to gain entrance. A 2011 survey conducted by the Korean Culture and Information Service reported that there were over 3 million active members of Hallyu fan clubs. An article by The Wall Street Journal indicated that K-pop's future staying power will be shaped by fans, whose online activities have evolved into "micro-businesses". K-pop groups commonly have dedicated fanclubs with a collective name and sometimes an assigned colour, to which they will release merchandise. For example, TVXQ fans are known as 'Cassiopeia', and their official colour is 'pearl red'. Some of the more popular groups have personalised light sticks for use at concerts; for example, Big Bang fans hold yellow crown-shaped light sticks. Fan clubs sometimes participate in charity events to support their idols, purchasing bags of 'fan rice' in order to show support. The rice bags are donated to those in need. According to Time, for one of Big Bang's shows, 12.7 tons of rice were donated from 50 fan clubs around the world. There are businesses in Korea dedicated to shipping rice from farmers to the venues. Another way that fan clubs show their devotion is sending lunch to idols during their schedules, and there are catering companies in South Korea specifically for this purpose. A unique feature of K-pop fandom is the 'fan chant'. When an idol group releases a new song, fan clubs will organise a

K-Pop

fan chant and learn it so that they can chant parts of the song or an idols' names at parts of the song during live performances.

NOTES

Chapter Four

K-pop worldwide popularity

"For the sake of standing high as idols, we will continue to run" — Seventeen

Japan

Following the lifting of import and export restrictions between South Korea and Japan in place since WWII, BoA's debut Japanese album Listen to My Heart in 2002 was the first album by a Korean artist to debut at the top of the Japanese Oricon charts and become an

RIAJ-certified 'million-seller' in Japan. On January 16, 2008, TVXQ (known as Tohoshinki in Japan) also reached the top of the Oricon charts with their sixteenth Japanese single "Purple Line". This made them the first foreign and Korean male group to have a number-one single in Japan. Since then, the Japanese market has seen an influx of Korean pop acts such as SS501, Shinee, Super Junior, Big Bang, KARA and Girls' Generation. In 2011, it was reported that the total sales for K-pop artists' increased 22.3% between 2010–2011 in Japan. Some Korean artists were in the top 10 selling artists of the year in Japan. With remaining tension between Japan and Korea, the import of Korean culture has been met with resistance, in the form of the 'Anti-Korean Wave'. One demonstration against the Korean Wave with roughly 500 participants was broadcast on Japan's Fuji TV to an Internet audience of over 120,000. However, the chairman of the Presidential Council on National Branding cites this resistance as proof of "how successful Korean Wave is." According to the Korea Foundation for International Culture Exchange's 'Korean Wave index', the top consumer in 2010 was Japan, in a list that also included Taiwan, China, Thailand, Indonesia, Vietnam, Malaysia and the Philippines.

A short encyclopedia

China

K-pop has yet to dominate the Chinese market, but there has been considerable success: in 2005, Rain held a concert in Beijing with 40,000 people in attendance. The Wonder Girls won an award in the 5th annual China Mobile Wireless Music Award for the highest digital sales for a foreign artist, with 5 million digital downloads in 2010. Entertainment companies often include Chinese members in idol groups with the aim of marketing to China; S.M. Entertainment's EXO-M was an example of this. Super Junior and their sub-group Super Junior-M have had successful results on the Kuang Nan Record, CCR and Hit Fm Taiwan music charts.

Taiwan

Despite sharing a similar past, the Taiwanese did not carry a positive sentiment towards South Korea after 1992, which is when South Korea broke off its diplomatic relationship with Taiwan in order to pursue one with mainland China. This changed in the early 2000s as the cultural dispersion of hallyu has contributed to the reconstruction of South Korea's image among the

Taiwanese. This change was in part prompted by the South Korean government, who wished to encourage goodwill between the two countries after the break of diplomacy. Now many Taiwanese have remarked that Korean popular music and Korean dramas has helped to foster a renewed interest and healthier relationship with South Korea.

India

In the Indian state of Manipur, where separatists have banned Bollywood movies, consumers have turned to Korean popular culture for their entertainment needs. The BBC's correspondent Sanjoy Majumder reported that Korean entertainment products are mostly unlicensed copies smuggled in from neighbouring Burma, and are generally well received by the local population. This has led to the increasing use of Korean phrases in common parlance among young people. In order to capitalize on the popularity of K-pop in Manipur, many hairdressing salons have offered "Korean-style" cuts based on the hairstyles of K-pop boy bands. This wave of Korean popular culture is currently spreading from Manipur to the neighbouring state of Nagaland.

A short encyclopedia

Singapore

There is a thriving K-pop fanbase in Singapore, where idol groups, such as 2NE1, EXO and BTS, often hold concert tour dates. The popularity of K-pop alongside Korean dramas has influenced the beauty image of Singaporeans. Korean-style "straight eyebrows" have become quite popular among many Singaporean females and males of Chinese, Malay and Indian descent. Singaporean beauty salons have seen an increase in the number of customers interested in getting Korean-style "straight eyebrows" in recent years.

Malaysia

In Malaysia, among the three main ethnic groups- Malay, Chinese and Indian- many prefer to listen to music in their own languages, but the popularity of K-pop alongside Korean movies and TV dramas has become popular among all three ethnic groups, which Malaysian firms have capitalised upon. The popularity of K-pop has also resulted in politicians bringing K-pop idols to the country in order attract young voters.

K-Pop

North America

In 2006, Rain held sold-out concerts in New York and Las Vegas as part of his Rain's Coming World Tour. In 2009, the Wonder Girls became the first K-pop artist to debut on the Billboard Hot 100 singles chart. They went on to join the Jonas Brothers on the Jonas Brothers World Tour 2009. In 2010, they toured 20 cities in the United States, Canada and Mexico, and were named House of Blues "Artist of the Month" for June. In 2010, S.M. Entertainment held the SMTown Live '10 World Tour with dates in Los Angeles, Paris, Tokyo, and New York. The same year, during the 8th Annual Korean Music Festival, K-pop artists made their first appearances at the Hollywood Bowl. Notable K-pop concerts in the United States in 2011 include the KBS Concert at the New York Korea Festival, the K-Pop Masters Concert in Las Vegas, and the Korean Music Wave in Google, which was held at Google's headquarters in Mountain View, California. 2012 marked a breakthrough year for K-pop in North America. At the start of the year, Girls' Generation performed the English version of "The Boys" on the late night talk show The Late Show with David Letterman and also on the daytime talk show Live! with Kelly, becoming the first Korean musical act to perform on these shows, and the first Korean act to perform on syndicated television in the United States. In the same year, the group formed their first sub-unit, entitled Girls' Generation-TTS, or simply "TTS", composed of members Taeyeon, Tiffany, and Seohyun. The subgroup's debut EP, Twinkle, peaked at #126 on the Billboard 200. In May, SMTown returned to California again with the SMTown Live World Tour III in Anaheim. In August, as part of their New Evolution Global Tour, 2NE1 held their first American concert in the New York Metropolitan Area at the Prudential Center of Newark, New Jersey. In November, as part of their Alive Tour, Big Bang held their first solo concert in America, visiting the Honda Center in Los Angeles and the Prudential Center in Newark. The tickets sold out in only a few hours, and additional dates were added. On November 13, the American singer-songwriter Madonna and backup dancers performed "Gangnam Style" alongside PSY during a concert at Madison Square Garden in New York City. PSY later told reporters that his gig with Madonna had "topped his list of accomplishments". On January 29, 2013, Billboard, one of America's most popular music magazines, launched Billboard K-Town, an online column on its website that covered K-pop news, artists, concerts, and chart information. In March of that year, f(x) performed at the K-Pop Night Out at SXSW in Austin, Texas, alongside the The Geeks, who represented Korean rock. f(x) was the first K-pop group ever to perform at SXSW. Mnet hosted its Kcon event in NY and LA in July 2016.

Latin America

Many idol groups have loyal fanbases in Latin America. Since 2009, about 260 fan clubs with a total of over 20,000 and 8,000 active members have been formed in Chile and Peru respectively. In 2011, the United Cube Concert was held in São Paulo, shortly after the second round of the first K-Pop Cover Dance Festival was held in Brazil, with MBLAQ as judges. In March 2012, JYJ performed in Chile and Peru. When the group arrived at the Jorge Chávez International Airport in Peru for the JYJ World Tour Concert, they were escorted by airport security officials through a private exit due to safety reasons concerning the large number of fans (over 3,000). At the Explanada Sur del Estadio Monumental in Lima, some fans camped out for days in to see JYJ. In April, Caracol TV and Arirang TV jointly aired a K-pop reality show in Colombia. In September, Junsu became the first K-pop idol to perform solo in Brazil and Mexico, after the Wonder Girls in Monterrey in 2009. The concerts sold out well in advance. That year there were 70 K-pop fan clubs in Mexico, with at least 60,000 members altogether. In January 2014, Kim Hyung-jun performed in Peru, Chile, and Bolivia, becoming the first K-pop idol to perform in Bolivia. The tour proved his popularity in the continent as both fans and the media followed him everywhere he went, causing traffic on the roads and police to be called to maintain safety. Fans were also seen pitching their tents outside the concert venue for days before the actual concert.

Europe

In 2010, both the SMTown Live '10 World Tour and the Super Junior Super Show 4 Tour were held in Paris. In February 2011, Teen Top performed at the Apolo concert hall in Barcelona. In May, Rain became the first K-pop artist to perform in Germany, during the Dresden Music Festival. JYJ also performed in both Berlin and

Barcelona. Big Bang flew to Belfast and won the Best Worldwide Act during the 2011 MTV EMAs in Northern Ireland. In Poland, the K-pop Star Exhibition was held in the Warsaw Korean Culture Center. K-pop also saw a surge in popularity in Russia, where 57 dance teams took part in the K-pop Cover Dance Festival. During the second round of the competition, SHINee flew to Moscow as judges, also performing to Russian fans. The following year, Russian youths launched K-Plus, a Korean culture magazine, and the number of Russian K-pop fans was reported at 50,000. In February 2012, BEAST held their Beautiful Show in Berlin. According to the Berliner Zeitung, many fans who attended were not just from Germany but also from neighbouring countries such as France and Switzerland. Also in February, the Music Bank World Tour drew more than 10,000 fans to the Palais Omnisports de Paris-Bercy. That year, artists such as Beast and 4Minute performed during the United Cube Concert in London, where the MBC Korean Culture Festival was also held. When SHINee arrived at the London Heathrow Airport for a concert at the Odeon West End in the same year, part of the airport became temporarily overrun by frenzied fans. The reservation system of the Odeon West End crashed for the first time one minute after ticket sales began as the concert drew an unexpectedly large response. At this time, SHINee also held a 30-minute performance at the Abbey Road Studio. The ticket demand for this performance was so high that fashion magazine Elle gave away forty tickets through a lottery, and the performance was also televised in Japan through six different channels. Also in 2012, Big Bang won the Best Fan category in the Italian TRL Awards. 2014 saw a continued rise in the popularity of K-pop in Russia. On February 3, Park Jung-min became the first ever Korean singer to hold a solo concert in Moscow.

Middle East and Africa

K-pop has become increasingly popular across the Middle East and Africa over recent years, particularly among younger fans. In July 2011, Israeli fans met South Korea's Ambassador to Israel, Ma Young-sam, and traveled to Paris for the SMTown Live '10 World Tour in Europe. According to Dr. Nissim Atmazgin, a professor of East Asian Studies at Hebrew University of Jerusalem, "Many young people look at K-pop as culture capital-something that makes them stand out from the crowd." As of 2012, there are over 5,000 K-pop fans in Israel and

3,000 in the Palestinian territories. Some dedicated Israeli and Palestinian fans see themselves as "cultural missionaries" and actively introduce K-pop to their friends and relatives, further spreading the Hallyu wave within their communities. In 2012, the number of fans in Turkey surpassed 100,000, reaching 150,000 in 2013. ZE:A appeared for a fan meet-and-greet session in Dubai and a concert in Abu Dhabi. In Cairo, hundreds of fans went to Maadi Library's stage theater to see the final round of the K-POP Korean Song Festival, organised by the Korean Embassy.

NOTES

A short encyclopedia

Chapter Five

Did you know that...?
20 interesting facts about K-pop

1. February 2006: Rain holds two sold-out performances at Madison Square Garden, New York.
2. May 2007: Rain is the first K-pop artist to perform at Japan's biggest concert hall, the Tokyo Dome; the 40,000 tickets sell within two days of sale.
3. October 2009: Wonder Girls enter the US Billboard Hot 100 single chart with "Nobody", widely noted for the viral spread of its music video.

4. December 2009: Wonder Girls are the first K-pop artist to perform on U.S. prime-time television when they appear on Fox's So You Think You Can Dance on December 9.

5. September 2010: S.M. Entertainment holds its first concert outside of Asia, the SMTown Live '10 World Tour at the Staples Center in Los Angeles, which grosses over US$1 million and is 9th on the Billboard Boxscore Chart. It precedes two sold-out concerts at Le Zénith in Paris few months later.

6. November 2011: Big Bang wins the 2011 MTV EMA for Best Worldwide Act.

7. February 2012: Girls' Generation appears on U.S. television, on the Late Show with David Letterman and Live! with Kelly on January 31 and February 1, 2012, where they perform remixes of the English version of their song "The Boys".

8. March 2012: After becoming the first K-pop band to enter the Billboard 200 record chart with their album Alive at #150, Big Bang commences their Alive Tour in 25 cities worldwide, including cities in the U.S., Peru, and the U.K. The tour ends in early 2013, having been attended by 800,000 concert-goers around the world.

9. August 2012: 2NE1 holds their New Evolution Concert at the Nokia Theatre in Los Angeles, ranking 29th on Billboard's Current Box Score.

A short encyclopedia

10. November 2012: Psy's "Gangnam Style" becomes the most viewed video on YouTube, and the first to reach one billion views. The video is also awarded the MTV Europe Music Award for Best Video.

11. March 2013: f(x) becomes the first K-pop group to perform at SXSW, during the K-Pop Night Out at SXSW in Austin, Texas.

12. April 2013: Super Junior extends their Super Show 5 Tour to Buenos Aires, São Paulo, Santiago and Lima, making it the largest K-pop tour in South America yet.

13. August 2013: TVXQ concludes their Live Tour 2013: Time with two performances at the Nissan Stadium in Japan, to a total 140,000 fans. They were the first foreign artists and the fourth musical artist overall to perform at the venue.

14. November 2013: Girls' Generation is awarded Video of the Year at the 2013 YouTube Music Awards for "I Got a Boy".

15. August 2014: Microsoft uses 2NE1's single "I Am The Best" on an international advertisement for the Surface Pro 3.

16. December 2014: 2NE1's Crush is the only album by an Asian artist listed on Fuse TV's 40 Best Albums Of 2014 and Rolling Stone's 20 Best Pop Albums of 2014. Crush is also the first ever K-pop entry on Billboard's year-end World Albums chart, ranking 11th.

17. April 2015-March 2016: Big Bang's MADE World Tour gathers 1.5 million fans around the world, making it the largest world tour by any Korean act, including the most attended concert tour by a foreign act in China and Japan and the most attended concert tour by a Korean act in the United States, Australia and Canada.
18. November 2015: BTS's album The Most Beautiful Moment In Life, Part 2 charts at number one on the Billboard World Albums Chart and remains in the top ten for eleven weeks.
19. August 2015: Super Junior is the first Asian artist who won International Artist at the Teen Choice Awards and "Best Fandom".
20. October 2016: BTS's album Wings becomes the first Korean album to chart in the UK Album Charts, reaching #62, and the highest charting and best selling K-pop album in the Billboard 200. They also became the first Korean artist to have three entries on the Billboard 200 and first K-pop act to have an entry for more than one week on the Billboard 200.

A short encyclopedia

Korean Pop stars

2000

- Papaya
- 5tion

2001

- Jewelry
- KISS.
- M.I.L.K
- jtL
- Epik High

2002

- Sugar
- Black Beat
- Shinvi
- Leessang
- LUV
- Isak N Jiyeon
- Moon Child (MC the Max)

2003

- Big Mama
- Dynamic Duo
- Brown Eyed Soul
- Buzz

K-POP

- TVXQ

2004

- SG Wannabe
- V.O.S
- TRAX

2005

- The Grace
- SS501
- Gavy NJ
- Super Junior
- Paran

2006

- SeeYa
- Brown Eyed Girls
- Untouchable
- Big Bang
- Super Junior-K.R.Y.

2007

- Wonder Girls
- Kara
- F.T. Island
- Girls' Generation
- 8eight
- Sunny Hill
- Supernova
- Tritops
- Super Junior-T

2008

- Davichi
- Double S 301
- Mighty Mouth
- Shinee
- Super Junior-M
- Super Junior-H
- 2AM
- 2PM
- U-KISS

2009

- 2NE1
- 4Minute
- After School
- Beast
- f(x)
- JQT
- MBLAQ
- Rainbow

A short encyclopedia

- Secret
- SHU-I
- T-ara
- CNBLUE
- December

2010

- APeace
- Coed School
- DMTN
- F.Cuz
- Girl's Day
- GD&TOP
- GP Basic
- Infinite
- JYJ
- Led Apple
- Miss A
- Nine Muses
- Orange Caramel
- Sistar
- Teen Top
- The Boss
- ZE:A

2011

- AA
- APink
- B1A4
- Blady
- Block B
- Boyfriend
- Brave Girls
- C-Real
- Chocolat
- Dal Shabet
- F-ve Dolls
- M&D
- M.I.B
- My Name
- N-Sonic
- N-Train
- RaNia
- Sistar19
- Stellar
- Super Junior-D&E
- Trouble Maker

2012

- 100%
- 15&
- 24K
- A-Jax
- AOA
- B.A.P
- Big Star
- BtoB
- C-Clown
- Crayon Pop
- Cross Gene
- D-Unit
- EvoL
- EXID

43

K-POP

- EXO
- Fiestar
- Gangkiz
- Girls' Generation-TTS
- Glam
- Hello Venus
- JJ Project
- Lunafly
- Mr. Mr.
- NU'EST
- Phantom
- Puretty
- She'z
- Skarf
- Spica
- Sunny Days
- Tahiti
- Tasty
- The SeeYa
- Tiny-G
- Two X
- VIXX

2013

- 2Yoon
- AlphaBat
- AOA Black
- Bestie
- Boys Republic
- BTS
- GI
- History
- Infinite H
- Ladies' Code
- LC9
- M.Pire
- NOM
- QBS
- Royal Pirates
- Speed
- T-ara N4
- Topp Dogg
- Wassup

2014

- 2000 Won
- 4L
- 4Ten
- 5urprise
- Akdong Musician
- Almeng
- Badkiz
- Berry Good
- Bigflo
- Bob Girls
- BTL
- D.Holic
- GD X Taeyang
- Got7
- High4
- Hi Suhyun
- HeartB
- Infinite F
- JJCC
- K-Much
- Laboum
- Lovelyz
- Madtown
- Mamamoo

A short encyclopedia

- Melody Day
- Minx
- Play the Siren
- Red Velvet
- Sonamoo

- ToHeart
- Uniq
- Wings
- Winner

2 0 1 5

- April
- Bambino
- Bastarz
- Big Brain
- CLC
- Cupid
- Day6
- DIA
- GFriend
- iKon
- Monsta X

- N.Flying
- Oh My Girl
- Playback
- Romeo
- Rubber Soul
- Seventeen
- Snuper
- Twice
- Unicorn
- UP10TION
- VIXX LR

2 0 1 6

- AOA Cream
- Astro
- AxisB
- Black Pink
- Boys24
- C.I.V.A
- Cosmic Girls
- EXO-CBX
- Gugudan
- I.B.I
- I.O.I

- Imfact
- K.A.R.D
- KNK
- MASC
- MOBB
- NCT
- Nine Muses A
- Pentagon
- SF9
- Victon
- Vromance

2 0 1 7

- Dream Catcher
- LOONA

45

NOTES

....
....
....
....
....
....
....
....

A short encyclopedia

K-pop artists dictionary

A
Ailee
Ajoo
Alexander Lee Eusebio

Ali
Amber Liu (f(x))

B
Bada
Bae Suzy (Miss A)
Bae Seul-ki
Baek Ji-young
Bang Yong Guk (B.A.P)
Bi (Rain)
Baro (B1A4)
Bizniz
BoA

Byul
Byun Baek-hyun (EXO)
Brian Joo
Baek A-yeon
Boom
Bora (Sistar)
Bang Cheol Yong (MBLAQ)

C
Chae Jung-an
Chae Yeon
Chen (EXO)
Cho Yong-pil
CNU (B1A4)
Choi Minho (Shinee)
Choi Sulli (f(x))
Cho Kyuhyun (Super Junior)

Choi Siwon (Super Junior)
Choi Soo-young (Girls' Generation)
Choi Min-hwan (F.T. Island)
Choi Jong-hoon (F.T. Island)
Crush_(singer)

D

Dae Sung (Big Bang)
Dana
Dara (2NE1)
Do Kyung-soo (EXO)

Dean_(South_Korean_singer)
Dok2
Drunken Tiger

E

Eru
Eugene
Eunhyuk (Super Junior)

Eun Ji Won
E.via
Eric Nam

F

Fat Cat

G

G.NA
Gary (Leessang)
Gil Seong-joon (Leessang)
Gummy
G-Dragon (Big Bang)

Goo Ha-ra (Kara)
Gain (Brown Eyed Girls)
G.O (singer) (MBLAQ)
Gongchan (B1A4)

H

Han Seungyeon (Kara)
Ham Eun-jeong (T-ara)
Han Sunhwa (Secret)
Ha Ji-won
Haha
Henry Lau (Super Junior M)
Heo Ga Yoon (4Minute)
Heo Young Saeng (SS501)
Heo Young-ji (Kara)
Hong Jin-Young
Hong Kyung Min

A short encyclopedia

Hoon (U-KISS)
Hyolyn (Sistar)
Hyomin (T-ara)
Hyun Bin
Huh Gak
Hwangbo (Chakra)
Hwang Chansung (2PM)
Tiffany Hwang (Girls' Generation)
Hwanhee
Hwayobi
Hyun Young
Hyelim (Wonder Girls)

I

Im Chang-jung
Im Yoona (Girls' Generation)
Insooni
IU
Ivy

J

J
JB (JJ Project)
Jr. (JJ Project)
Jang Dong-woo (Infinite)
Jang Keun-suk
Jang Hyun-seung (Beast)
Jang Na-ra
Jang Woo Hyuk
Jang Wooyoung (2PM)
Jang Yun-jeong
Jeon Boram (T-ara)
Jeon Hye Bin
Jia (Miss A)
Jeon Ji Yoon (4Minute)
Jeong Jinwoon (2AM)
Jessica Jung
J-Min
Jo Eun Byul
Jo Kwon (2AM)
Jo Sungmo
JOO
Joy (Red Velvet)
John Park
Jonghyun (Shinee)
Joo Hyun-Mi
Jun Jin
Jun Hyoseong (Secret)
Jun.K (2PM)
Jung Daehyun (B.A.P)
Jung Hana (Secret)
Jinyoung (B1A4)
Nicole Jung (Kara)

49

K-Pop

Jung Yong-hwa
(CN Blue)

Juniel

K

K
Kai (EXO)
Kim Jungah (After School)
KCM
Kahi (entertainer)
Kan Mi-youn
Kang Min-hyuk (CN Blue)
Kang Seung-yoon (Winner)
Kang Sung-hoon
Kangin (Super Junior)
Kangta
Key (Shinee)
Kibum (Super Junior)
Kim Ah-joong
Kim Bum
Kim Bum-soo
Kim C
Kim Dong-ryool
Kim Dong-wan
Kim Gun-mo
Kim Heechul (Super Junior), (M&D)
Kim Himchan (B.A.P)
Kim Hyoyeon (Girls' Generation)
Kim Hyuna (4Minute)
Kim Hyun-joong (SS501)
Kim Hyung-jun (SS501)
Kim Jaejoong (JYJ)
Kim Jong-kook
Kim Joon (T-Max)
Kim Junsu (JYJ)
Kim Kyu-jong (SS501)
Kim Kyung-ho
Kim Myung-soo (Infinite)
Kim Ryeowook (Super Junior)
Kim Tae-woo
Kim Tae-yeon (Girls' Generation)
Kim Seol-hyun (AOA)
Kim Soo-hyun
Kim Sung-kyu (Infinite)

A short encyclopedia

Kim Taeyeon (Girls' Generation)
Kim Yeonji (SeeYa)
Kwon So-hyun (4Minute)
Kim Young-sook)

Krystal Jung (f(x))
Kwon Mina (AOA)
Kwon Yuri (Girls' Generation)
K.Will

L

Lay (EXO)
Lee Jooyeon (After School)
Lee Chae-rin (2NE1)
Lee Dong-gun
Lee Donghae (Super Junior)
Lee Gi-kwang (Beast)
Lee Min-young (Miss A)
Lee Hi
Lee Howon (Infinite)
Lee Hong-gi (F.T. Island)
Lee Hyori (Fin.K.L)
Lee Hyun
Lee Jae-jin (F.T. Island)
Lee Jae-won
Lee Ji-hoon
Lee Jin (Fin.K.L)

Lee Jong-hyun (CN Blue)
Lee Joon (MBLAQ)
Lee Junho (2PM)
Lee Jung
Lee Jung-hyun
Lee Joon-gi
Lee Ki-chan
Lee Min-ho
Lee Min-woo
Lee Seung-hoon (Winner)
Lee Seung-chul
Lee Seung-gi
Lee Seung-hyun (Bigbang)
Lee Soo-young
Lee Sora
Lee Sung-jong (Infinite)
Lee Sungmin (Super Junior)
Lee Sung-yeol (Infinite)

Lee Tae-min (Shinee)
Leeteuk (Super Junior)
Lena Park

Lexy
Lim Jeong-hee
Luna (singer) (f(x))
Lyn

M

MC Mong
MC Sniper
Min Hae Kyung
Min Hyorin
Min Hyuk (CNBLUE)
Minzy (2NE1)

Mina
Minwoo
Moon Ga-young
Moon Hee Jun
Moon Jong Up (B.A.P)

N

Nam Ji-hyun (4Minute)
Nam Woo-hyun (INFINITE)
Nana (After School)
Narsha

Nichkhun Horvejkul (2PM)
Nicole (Kara)
Nicky Lee
No Minwoo
NS Yoon-G

O

Oh Se-hun (EXO)
Onew (Shinee)

Outsider

P

Park Bom (2NE1)
Park Chan-yeol (EXO)
Park Choa (AOA)
Park Gyu-ri (Kara)
Park Jung-ah (Jewelry)

Park Jung-min (SS501)
Park Ji-yeon (T-ara)
Park Ji-yoon
Park Jin-young
Park Junyoung
Park Yong-ha

A short encyclopedia

Jay Park
Park Shin-hye
Park Myeong-su

Park Soyeon (T-ara)
Psy

Q

Qri (T-ara)

R

Raina (After School)
Rain
Rap Monster
Roh Ji Hoon

Ryu Si-won
Ryu Hwayoung
Ryu Hyoyoung (Co-ed)(5dolls)

S

Sandeul (B1A4)
Se7en
Seo Joohyun (Girls' Generation)
Seo Hyo-rim
Seo In-guk
Seo In-young
Seo Ji-young
Seo Yuna (AOA)
Seomoon Tak
Seo Taiji
Seungho (MBLAQ)
Shim Changmin
Shim Eun-jin
Shin Dongho (U-KISS)
Shin Dong-hee (Super Junior)
Shin Hae-chul

Shin Hye-jeong (AOA)
Shin Hye-sung
Shin Ji
Shin Ji-min (AOA)
Shin Seung-hun
Shoo (S.E.S.)
Sim Soo-bong
So Chan-whee
Sohee (Wonder Girls)
Solbi
Son Dam-bi
Son Dong-woon (Beast)
Son Hoyoung
Song Jieun (Secret)
Song Ji-hyo
Song Joong-ki

53

K-POP

Song Min-ho (Winner)
Song Seung-hyun (F.T. Island)
Sunny (Girls' Generation)

Suho (EXO)
Sung Si-kyung
Sung Yu-ri

T

T.O.P (Big Bang)
Tablo (Epik High)
Tae Bin
Taecyeon (2PM)
Tae Jin Ah
Taegoon

Taeyang (Big Bang)
Tasha Reid
Tim
Tony An
Thunder (MBLAQ)

U

Uee (After School)
U;Nee

Uhm Jung-hwa

V

Victoria Song (f(x))

W

Wax
Wendy (Red Velvet)
Wheesung

Wang Fei Fei (Miss A)
Woo Sung-hyun (U-KISS)

X

Xiumin (EXO)

Y

Yang Hyun-suk
Yang Yo-seob
Yesung (Super Junior)
Yim Jae-beom

(Beast)
Yeon Woo
Yoo Ara (Hello Venus)
Yoo Chae-yeong

A short encyclopedia

Yoo Seung-jun
Yoo Young-jae (B.A.P)
Yoon Eun-hye
Yoon Mi-rae
Yong Jun-hyung (Beast)
Yoochun (JYJ)
You Hee-yeol
Younha

Yubin (Wonder Girls)
Yoo Seung-ho
Yunho (TVXQ)
Yoon Doo-joon (Beast)
Yeeun (Wonder Girls)
Yangpa

Z

Zelo (B.A.P)
Zhou Mi (Super Junior-M)

Zia
Zion.T

NOTES

K-Pop

A short encyclopedia

sources

Hartong, Jan Laurens (2006). Musical Terms Worldwide: A Companion for the Musical Explorer. Semar Publishers. ISBN 978-88-7778-090-4.

Holden, Todd Joseph Miles; Scrase, Timothy J. (2006). Medi@sia: Global Media/tion In and Out of Context. Taylor & Francis. ISBN 978-0-415-37155-1.

Kim, Myung Oak; Jaffe, Sam (2010). The New Korea: An Inside Look at South Korea's Economic Rise. AMACOM Div American Mgmt Assn. ISBN 978-0-8144-1489-7.

K-Pop: A New Force in Pop Music (PDF) (Korean Culture No. 2 ed.). Korean Culture and Information Service; Ministry of Culture, Sports and Tourism. 2011. ISBN 978-89-7375-166-2.

Meza, X. V., & Park, H. W. (2015). Globalization of cultural products: a webometric analysis of Kpop in Spanish-speaking countries. *Quality & Quantity*, 49(4), 1345-1360.

Russell, Mark James (2014). K-POP Now! The Korean Music Revolution. Tuttle Publishing. ISBN 978-4805313008

Wikipedia, the Free encyclopedia : https://en.wikipedia.org/wiki/K-pop

K-Pop

© 2017, Park, Jee-Eun
Edition : Books on Demand,
12 / 14 rond point des champs Elysées, 75008 Paris
Impression : BoD - Books on Demand Norderstedt, Allemagne
ISBN : 9782322132904
Dépôt légal : Janvier 2017